THE
GREAT AWAKENING

AHMED HULUSI

www.ahmedhulusi.org/en/

As with all my works, this book is not copyrighted.
As long as it remains faithful to the original,
it may be freely printed, reproduced, published and translated.
For the knowledge of ALLAH, there is no recompense.

THE
GREAT AWAKENING

AHMED HULUSI
www.ahmedhulusi.org/en/

Translated by ALIYA ATALAY

ABOUT THE COVER

The black background of the front cover represents darkness and ignorance, while the white color of the letters represents light and knowledge.

The image is a Kufi calligraphy of the Word of Unity: *"La ilaha illallah; Muhammad Rasulullah"* which means,

"There is no concept such as 'god', there is only that which is denoted by the name Allah, and **Muhammad (SAW)** is the *Rasul* of this understanding."

The placement of the calligraphy, being on top and above everything else on the page, is a symbolic representation of the predominant importance this understanding holds in the author's life.

The green light, reflecting from the window of the Word of Unity, opens up from the darkness into luminosity to illustrate the light of Allah's *Rasul*. This light is embodied in the book's title through the author's pen and concretized as the color white, to depict the enlightenment the author aims to attain in this field. As the knowledge of Allah's *Rasul* disseminates, those who are able to evaluate this knowledge attain enlightenment, which is represented by the white background of the back cover.

"Can one who knows be equal to one who does not know?"

Quran 39:9

"To question is half of knowledge"

Muhammad (saw)

"Those who cannot see can never know what it's like for those who can see! Therefore, let not the accusations of the unseeing deter those with sight..."

Ahmed Hulusi

CONTENTS

TRANSLATOR'S NOTE

This book recapitulates the primary and most essential teaching of Sufism – that everything in existence is a reflection of the divine, a manifestation of the Names of Allah.

When one begins to see the world through this lens, that is, not just as a plane of physical entities, but as the grand display of divine manifestations, something profound takes place. The notion of judgment and criticism drops completely. If one concludes that everything and everyone is the manifestation of the One – and there is no other – then, quite conspicuously, one's very being is also an expression of no other than this One. If the invisible field of intelligence and energy, what scientists today call nonlocality, connects everything to everything and everyone else in the universe, then judging any form is judging the Divine One, or rather, judging one's core being.

Observing existence from this perspective, one begins to appreciate all forms and reflections of the One, oblivious of conditioned beliefs, prejudices, labels and identifications.

Written in 1967, in his early twenties, this book evinces the profound insight of Ahmed Hulusi, calling the reader once again, to reassess the validity of their assumed reality within the reflections of the One.

Aliya Atalay
Istanbul, 2013

1

INTRODUCTION

Dear reader...

Much has been said to date – some have written according to what they heard, understood and discerned; some found it unnecessary to say so much and wanted to express everything with one word... Some accepted the Truth, some denied... But the denial of the deniers only provided more evidence to the Truth...

Some spent their time criticizing and accusing each other, claiming the 'other' was in the wrong and they were the 'protectors' – as if there were a need for protection... While some said, "No matter how separate you see yourselves, we are all one"...

We can divide all humans into two general categories. Those who sincerely think about others as much as they think of themselves, and those who act only out of personal gain and vested interest... But judging or criticizing others based on their actions is not something we do. How can we, when the verse plainly says:

"Say, 'Everyone acts according to his own creation program (natural disposition; fitrah).**' This is why your Rabb** (who is the *Fatir*) **knows best who is on the right path!"**[1]

Success is from Allah, the Rabb of the worlds.

---

[1] Quran 17:84

3

4

FROM THE SHELL TO THE CORE

Dear reader...

These lines were written in a state of tranquility and bliss, purified from all interests of benefit, with the intention to help those who aspire to reach the 'reality' to have a better understanding of certain Truths.

I would like to begin with the following statement:

"They, who deny and criticize you, are those who cannot comprehend the reality, nor can they understand you... But those who comprehend the Truth neither criticize nor see any faults in anyone."

We shall overcome many milestones, go through various stations, and reach the reality determined by our patience.

When one relinquishes his desires of interest, he reaches the station of divine governance, and when he is pleased with what comes his way, he reaches the state of a pleased servant...

The station of divine governance (amr^2) is free from all desires and mechanisms that pertain to the material world, such as eating, drinking and sleeping...

---

[2] The dimension of angelic forces.

Based on the command of the One, our Master has practiced and advised, "Address each person according to his intellect!"

Thus, those of knowledge and discernment during the time of Risalah and afterwards, have always sought to express certain Truths via metaphors and symbols. They did not attempt to explain the naked Truth, or disclose and interpret the secrets to which they had insight, but relayed it to the next person of authenticity.

In addressing those who respond to the call, "Read and try to comprehend! If you really want to have a say, first know yourself!" I would like to draw attention to the Truth that there is absolutely no difference among the creation in the sight of those who attain the reality... Indeed, all forms of existence are uniquely special.

Dear reader, know that...

Concepts and deviations such as 'valuable' and 'invaluable' are merely according to created/constructed identities! In the sight of the Creator there is only the creation. Good and bad are relative and their validity is only in respect to the creation. In the sight of the Creator, they are all one!

Man evolves to the extent that he can forego his personal 'relative' perceptions and ideas, which are totally relative, and annihilates himself in the sight of Allah!

Thus, the perfect man is one who neither sees nor seeks any flaws or defects in the creation. For everyone acts according to their ability to think and comprehend, and faces the consequences of their actions thusly.

We know these words will not convert the fixed beliefs and opinions of those whose natural dispositions does not allow. But it may aid those who are looking for and are destined to reach their essential reality to return to the origin of being.

The Rasul of Allah (saw) says, **"O Allah, there is none to prevent what You give and none can make You give when You prevent, and**

none can refuse Your command! You are powerful (Qadir) **over all things and do as You will!"**[3]

Dear reader, know that…

There is not a single creation that has not been created as perfect! Those who claim otherwise only reveal their limited perception. All creations are perfect, because their beauty is in respect to their creational purpose. People label things good and bad according to what suits and benefits them. They then try to justify this by saying, "Allah created both the beautiful and the ugly, so people can take a lesson and be either grateful or patient." This may be true, yet only based on this understanding and perception, not in the absolute sense.

The absolute Truth is that the Creator has created all things upon beauty and perfection. One needs only to take off their colored lens and observe the Truth with naked eyes. Only then can things be appreciated for what they truly are.

Our way is not the way of division, but the way of absolute oneness. There is no diversion on this path; one who wants to attain or comprehend the Truth cannot differentiate among creation.

The mature one is he who observes existence with the eyes of the Divine Truth (*haqq*) and refrains from observing differences among the created.

We have been commanded to not betray the things with which we have been entrusted, and to treat them in the best conduct, as they deserve to be treated. How then can one make division, and label and judge people and things? Our duty is to recognize and obey the divine commands, and to help others as best as possible with kindness and compassion.

If there is difference among them in the sight of the Creator, then surely the judgment is His. What is incumbent upon us is to know our place and not transgress.

The next step after transcending the differences among creation is to be an instrument for giving. "In every state and condition, try to be a

---

[3] Sahih Muslim, Sahih Bukhari

giver!" And never expect or even consider a return. In fact, do not even assume a return from the Creator. Simply try to be an instrument for the good at every instance in your life, unrequitedly.

Do not afflict or be a cause for harm upon others. Always consider their purpose of existence. Aspire to be a cause for good and benefit. And try to reach such an elevated state that you prefer something that is seemingly as insignificant as an insect or leaf to yourself.

Reach such a level of renunciation and sacrifice that you become able to share your slice of bread with one who is full but who desires it, even if you have been hungry for days. And not just your worldly possessions, but give also the gains and benefits of all your worship to the needy without taking any share in it. This is the way to dissociate yourself, or your identity, from your doings.

Work consistently. But let not this striving be for yourself, but to help creation, the trust of the Creator, so that good may reach them.

While most people choose their friends based on vested interests, choose a friend who is omnipotent, not in need of the help of anything that is created. But who is not in need of anything that is created other than the Creator? Indeed, make Him your point of turning. Present your needs to Him.

Think, think and think again, even if you can't reach the reality of your thoughts, at least join the rank of those who think.

If you are unable to discern the wisdom behind what transpires, at least refrain from objecting and wait until things come to an eventuality, lest you show an impulsive and imprudent reaction. Neither commit an offence, nor put yourself in a position where you have to ask for forgiveness.

Ambition resulting from one's own desires become one's devil. One who is devoid of desire will also be devoid of such pursuits; leaving their devil in a state of submission, rendering their devil Muslim! Since one who attains this state will be cleansed from vested interests, he will neither cause nor be afflicted by harm. For people usually favor those from whom they can benefit, and if they are far from the reality, they usually accredit the gift to the giver. But in Truth, both the giver and the One who causes the act of giving is Him! Therefore, one should neither be proud of nor rely on anything they own or possess, not even their faith, let alone their material possessions and friends and family. While you think you are faithful, a small and seemingly insignificant situation may easily evaporate your faith away.

The Rasul of Allah (saw) says, **"I swear by Allah, besides whom there is no god, that one of you acts like the people of Paradise until there remains between him and Paradise the distance of a cubit, when suddenly the writing of destiny overcomes him and he begins to act like the people of hell. And another one acts like the people of hell, until there remains between him and hell the distance of a cubit, when the writing of destiny overcomes him and he begins to act like the people of Paradise and thus enters Paradise!"**[4]

Therefore, do not boast with or rely on anything of yourself in this short and transient lifetime…

Repent to the Creator frequently, but not just with your tongue. True repentance is the acknowledgement of and feeling regret for one's mistakes. This is why the Rasul of Allah (saw) says, **"Repentance is penitence."**[5]

If your mistake entails an affliction you have caused upon another creation, then try to compensate for the harm you caused and ask for their forgiveness. The most eminent of acts is to be a cause for one's happiness through an act of benevolence. To attend to the needs of an ill person for a single hour during the night is far greater than thousands of night prayers. For, while engaging in worship is a recommendation in one's spare time, attending to someone who is in need is an obligation. So try, in the sight of the Creator, to be in service to creation, in fulfilling their purpose of existence. The value of a person in the sight of people is in respect to their closeness to the Creator… So make your closeness and turning point be to your Rabb, your essence. What matters is not your appearance, looks, age, etc., but your knowledge and discernment of the reality. So, think about what time has contributed to you in terms your ability to comprehend the Truth.

---

[4] Sahih Muslim
[5] Ibn Majah

9

Dear reader, know that…

The time has come for everyone to unite in the way of absolute oneness and unity. There is no diversion of sects and religions on this way. All colors on this path are united. Oblivious of one's religious or social background, if their purpose is to be in service to Allah and humanity, they are the travelers of this path. The only condition of this way is to aid creation, in every circumstance and situation, to reach the Truth and to be a cause for good to reach them.

The travelers of this path cannot be overcome by pride, arrogance, conceitedness or laziness. For they are those who have made service their duty; they prefer others to themselves. They are far from falsity and superstitions. They work only for the greater good of humanity. Rather than squandering their time on useless things, they spend it in service to humanity. None among the creation is wealthier than them; they have wings! They listen to and empathize with everyone in respect to their creational purpose, yet they hear nothing but the call of the Truth.

They know that everything in existence comprises the reflections of the Creator. And they also know that reflections are subject to constant change and none can know how the next reflection will take place.

"At every instance HU (the Absolute Essence of Existence) **manifests Himself in yet another way!"**[6]

Thus, they know that there is life in everything observable and unobservable. All is alive, all is full of life…

"There is nothing that does not exalt (*tasbih*) **Him with *hamd*** (evaluation of the corporeal worlds created with His Names, as He wills)! **But you do not perceive their functions!"**[7]

This Truth cannot be discerned by anyone other than those of comprehension! The Truth is covered by only two kinds of people. Those who are unaware of it, and hence cover it inadvertently, or those who conceal it consciously from those who wish to impugn and defame it.

---

[6] Quran 55:29
[7] Quran 17:44

Dear reader…

Hell is a state in which one's consciousness and body suffers, while heaven is a state of bliss. There is no firewood or coal therein. In today's terms, that which is referenced as hell is in fact the sun. Not in terms of its visible supra-atomic self, but in terms of its subatomic radial dimension. The earth will be pulled into the sun, which will expand until it reaches and engulfs Mars. This will cause the earth to evaporate! Those who cannot make it to the places of infinite pleasure, the sub-dimensions of the stars that are referenced as heavens, will be forever stuck and imprisoned in the sun. What is referenced in the Quran as '*Samum*', which is the poisonous waves of radiation emitted by the sun, will continually torture the holographic wave-bodies of those who will be stuck therein, causing them great suffering. The jinn of satanic qualities will also be here, and they will play with the feeble humans.

Some of the residents of hell will be the personifications of the deeds of the people. If we try to explain what the metaphors pertaining to hell actually mean it will be baffling and inconceivable. The life of heaven and hell are both reminiscent of the dream state. Both these words are only metaphoric references, which need to be construed, and that is not possible to do so here, at least not to its full extent.

The hadith **"Both the firewood and the coal** (fuel) **of hell is man"** and **"Allah created for His servants such things in paradise that no ear has heard, no eye has seen, and no mind can ever imagine…"**[8] allude to this.

"And their Rabb will have given them pure wine (the euphoric state caused by exposure to the reality).**"**[9]

This also means that their Rabb will enable them the experience of real love! As honey symbolizes faith, milk symbolizes *laduni* knowledge (knowledge pertaining to the potential of the Names comprising one's essence) while water is metaphoric of gnosis (*marifatullah*).

---

[8] Sahih Muslim
[9] Quran 76:21

Dear reader, know that...

There is the interpretation of the Quran, and then there is its actual meaning... The interpretation of the Quran is the expansion of its extrinsic meaning as a result of years of arduous study. Its actual meaning, on the other hand, can only be known by the 'intimates of the reality' - those who have been bestowed with knowledge from *Ind'Allah* (the forces that are revealed through dimensional emergence to consciousness from the Names of Allah that comprise one's essence). They know the meaning of every verse and hadith.

"And none can discern this except those who have reached the essence (the intimates of reality through whom Allah hears, sees and speaks; *ulul albab*).**"**[10]

'The intimates of the reality' are those who have been guided to the knowledge of the reality. With the knowledge disclosed to them by the Rabb of the worlds they inform us of the real meaning of each verse.

"Only Allah knows their (true and precise) **interpretation. Those who are grounded in knowledge** (deep contemplators) **say, 'We believe, all of it is from our Rabb.' And none can discern this except those who have reached the essence** (the intimates of the reality through whom Allah hears, sees and speaks; *ulul albab*).**"**[11]

These intimates of the reality are those who have been guided to *laduni* knowledge (the knowledge pertaining to the potential of the Names comprising one's essence). They live without any veils; they have attained the reality.

"The (tree's) **oil** (the observation of the reality in consciousness) **would almost glow even if untouched by fire** (active cleansing)...**"**[12]

This is a divine bestowal, a bounty...

"That is the favor of Allah; He bestows it upon whom He wills."[13]

And none can question why He does this.

---

[10] Quran 3:7
[11] Quran 3:7
[12] Quran 24:35
[13] Quran 5:54

"He is not questioned (called to account) **for what He does!"**[14]

There are some people who have merely heard of the ocean; all their knowledge is based on what they have heard. Then there are some who have seen it, but due to their inability to swim, they have only walked on the shore, perhaps gone in knee-deep. And then there are some who know how to swim and they swim out far. Yet beyond all of these, there are some who have almost become the ocean, they swim deep and far and discover new things all the time.

This is how people are in regards to real knowledge. Some have only heard of it, some read the Quran and suffice with fulfilling its orders and refraining from what has been forbidden. This is the case for the majority of the Muslims.

But then there are some who try harder and commit to mastering all of its intricate subtleties. They are referred to as the '*abrar*'.

There are others still, who are highly capacitated, and Allah bestows His favor on them. They too swim out far and deep and thus discover and discern the divine secrets. They are known as the '*muqarriboon*'. They are the chosen ones.

"Allah chooses for Himself whom He wills..."[15]

They think well and base their assumptions on perfection in regards to their Rabb! They act in accordance with the hadith Qudsi:

"I am as my servant assumes me to be."

And the verse:

"Indeed, certain assumptions are an offence (lead to or are an outcome of duality)!"**[16]

---

[14] Quran 21:23
[15] Quran 42:13
[16] Quran 49:12

Dear reader, know that...

The Creator is constantly providing innumerable provisions to His creation. Firstly, on the external level, He provides for your body with food and drink. Then He provides for your consciousness with knowledge. And then, through a new manifestation at every instance, He continues to provide for your material and spiritual bodies. We can continue to list the levels of provision, but for now let us suffice with these three. Every provision is best suited to the nature of the receiver, each time enabling it to evolve a little more and get closer to its essence. Though the provision may be general, each receives according to his capacity and skill. One with a greater plate will obviously have room for more. This depends on the capacity of the person.

"Allah gives provision (both limited sustenance for the corporeal life and infinite life sustenance pertaining to the realization of one's inner reality and its benefits) **to whom He wills without account..."**[17]

Rasulullah (saw) talks about the three different types of soil upon which rain falls. When it rains, it rains equally upon all different soils without discriminating among them. If rain falls upon stones it simply runs off them, for it is not in the nature of stones to absorb water. There are some soils that preserve water as pools or wells, and the people are able to drink from it, water their animals and crops with it, etc. And sometimes, it rains upon a soil that absorbs the water and gives forth various types of produce.

People are also of various types of nature. Some do not understand divine wisdom and warning, some benefit much from them, and some not only benefit but cause many others to benefit as well.

Which of these are you?

Dear reader, know that...

Your duty is to be beneficial both to yourself and to your surroundings. No one has remained on earth eternally. Every born being undergoes

---

[17] Quran 2:212

development according to its natural disposition and then at some point returns to its origin.

"Say, 'Everyone acts according to his own creation program (natural disposition; fitrah).'"[18]

The Rasul of Allah (saw) says, **"Everyone acts according to that for which he has been created and does the things which have been eased for him."**[19]

Hence, his life is shaped according to what he is to live.

But what if this person has lived a life contrary to the commands of his Rabb? What will happen to him?

Doubtlessly, different forms have been created for different states of existence. The nightingale for the rose garden, the dung beetle for the dung, the salamander for fire... Neither likes what the other likes; each is adversely different to one another... One burns in the fire the other thrives in, one can't stand the smell of roses, etc.... Like colors... They are all different...

So, whatever your essence is, you will engage in the deeds pertaining to that, and thus return to your essential reality. But there are some people of eminence who can unite the opposites! They have vast capacities with which they merge that seem to be in opposition with one another. In their sight, everything is one. There are no colors in their view. They are colorless. Yet they manifest according to the commands of Allah. They comprehend well the verse:

"Say: 'Allah' and let them amuse themselves in their empty discourse (their illusory world) **in which they are absorbed."**[20]

They know that everything observable is the reflection of the Creator. Even the attributes are reflections. And all of them are the reflections, or manifestations, of the single Being, Allah, the Akbar! Hence, one should not make any distinction among the created, the divine reflections... Is this not also the reason why the Quran asserts:

---

[18] Quran 17:84
[19] Faiz Al Qadeer
[20] Quran 6:91

"We make no distinction between (the ways in which the knowledge of Allah was revealed to) **His Rasuls..."**[21]

This is because all of them are from the same source!

What the eye observes as 'different' is due to the size and shape of the lamps, but those of true comprehension know well that regardless of these seeming differences, they all transmit the same electricity. Their external appearances are different because they have been designed as such, but their energy is all the same. The same electricity flows through them. But only those of insight can see this.

Thus far I have comprehensively explained how and why there is no difference among the created, the reflections of the One, if you have not grasped this as yet I urge you to do so today.

"And these examples (symbolic language) **We present to mankind so that they will contemplate."**[22]

But if you are still unable, then no doubt the Rabb does as He wills.

When the servant understands this simple Truth, he becomes pleased with his Rabb, and says, "Forgive me, if You will, or cause me to suffer; admit me to Your paradise, the state of bliss, if You will, or cast me into the suffering of hell. Everything is in service to You," and continues to engage in the *dhikr* (remembrance) of his Rabb. He contemplates the reflections and manifestations of his Rabb, refraining, however, from contemplating on His Absolute Essence (*dhat*) and claims, "He is Akbar (the Great)."

Yet he does not use the word 'Akbar' (the Great) in reference to His reflections, for he knows this word can pertain to Allah alone, His Absolute Essence. The reflection may be relatively great, but not 'the Great'. Thus, he understands the reality of the reflections of his Rabb. He neither denies any, nor makes any criticism, nor confines himself by them. Therefore, he knows only his Rabb and the Rasul (saw) as his essential reality.

---

[21] Quran 2:285
[22] Quran 59:21

"...Had Allah willed, He would surely have enabled the realization of the absolute reality to all of mankind!"[23]

But if He had, then how would all the other Divine Names have become manifest?

Did you not hear the hadith:

"I swear by Him in whose hand is my soul, if you were a people who did not commit sin, Allah would take you away and replace you with a people who would sin and then seek Allah's forgiveness so He could forgive them."[24]

Then he will reach the highest point of tolerance. He will no longer find anyone faulty nor any fault! However, he will not boast with this state, nor will he rely on it. For he will know that it is Allah who bestows this state to him. At this point, this 'colorless' person will say:

"Certainly, I have turned my face (my consciousness) **cleansed from the concept of a deity** (Hanif), **toward the Fatir** (He who creates everything programmed according to its purpose) **who created the heavens and the earth, and I am not of the dualists."**[25]

He will no longer have any desires nor any complaints regarding his state. How dare he when the command says:

"Let the one who is not pleased with my fate take for himself a god besides me!"[26]

Thus he becomes immediately pleased with his state and reflects the verse:

"Well-pleased is Allah with them, and well-pleased are they with Him (the reflections of divine qualities)..."[27]

---

[23] Quran 13:31
[24] Sahih Muslim (2687)
[25] Quran 6:79
[26] Tabarani
[27] Quran 98:8

Hadhrat Sa'd (salam upon him), the uncle of Rasulullah (saw), whose prayers were accepted without exception due to a powerful prayer of Rasulullah (saw), lost his sight in the last years of his life. They said to him, "Why don't you pray for your sight?" His response reflected a state not easily attainable by those of discernment. He said, "I love the decree of Allah more than I love my eyes!"

Such people reflect the knowledge and tolerance of the Rabb. They take precautions. Some say people of submission do not need to take precautions. But is their submission not their way of taking precautions?

Only they know that precautions are also from predestination!

That is, whether you have taken precautions or not is also the result of fate. But you can only know your fate after you have completed the action, and hence, no one can blame fate.

So, depending on what is due to transpire, you either take precautions or you don't. You will only understand this if you have been endowed with the program to do so.

"...He whose heart (essence) **Allah has expanded towards comprehending Islam..."**[28]

Dear reader...

After learning all of this, attempt to cleanse yourself. Start with:

"He who purifies (his consciousness) **has succeeded."**[29]

If you feel the tendency/inclination in your heart – for intention really means a heartfelt inclination – then know that this path will have been eased for you as necessitated by your destiny. So do not waste your valuable time on that which you will regret tomorrow!

---

[28] Quran 39:22
[29] Quran 91:9

"Remember (*dhikr*) the qualities of the Names comprising your essence, your Rabb, and seclude yourself to Him in complete devotion."[30]

"Allah chooses for Himself whom He wills and guides those who turn to Him to (realize their inner) **reality!"**[31]

Strive to be in this state. Strive so that you may turn to your essence with strength and be quick in your development. For you are on the right path; you have been given guidance as a result of your quest. Hands of support reach out to you from the inside and outside, didn't you read the book:

"And those who strive (against their egos) **to reach Us, We will surely enable them to reach Our ways** (by enabling them to realize their innermost essential reality)..."**[32]

Thus you will be guided to realize your innermost essential reality; the gates of understanding will have opened to you and you will have found the right path.

"Whoever is enabled by Allah to observe his innermost essential self, he is the one who reaches the reality!"[33]

After such discernment you need to be exceptionally careful not to fall into a state of duality and not confuse the cause for the causer, lest you inadvertently deify the cause!

"Do not turn to (assume the existence of) **a god** (exterior manifestations of power or your illusory self) **besides Allah."**[34]

Know that He does not like the dualists and does not forgive until one truly repents. More information on this can be obtained in *Muhammad's Allah*.

"Assuredly, duality is a great wrongdoing!"[35]

---

[30] Quran 73:8
[31] Quran 42:13
[32] Quran 29:69
[33] Quran 7:178
[34] Quran 28:88
[35] Quran 31:13

After this you will finally reach a state where you will no longer have an identity or any attachments. Only the Creator will remain – and His will.

In this state you will begin to observe the reality, the entire existence will disappear, only Allah will remain in your sight. You will no longer be able to blame anyone or find any faults. For all things that have come from non-existence will have become non-existent. Neither the world nor the hereafter will hold any validity to you anymore...

Your eyes will see, your ears will hear, your hands will grasp, your feet will walk, your tongue will speak only Him. You will have cleansed yourself of your illusory identity, you will have annihilated yourself in Him, in a state of full acceptance.

Be careful! This pleasure does not entail blind submission. There is no room for patience here. For patience denotes accepting and tolerating something against one's desire. Patience was encountered in previous stages, but in this stage there is nothing unpleasing! Whatever the Rabb has willed and created is beautiful and perfect. How can an artwork question its artist? When you reach this station you will no longer criticize or question anyone. Just like the Rasul of Allah (saw) who never once questioned or criticized Hadhrat Anas (ra) who served him for many years. For he knew what fate was. And this is the stage at which you will also begin to understand the mystery of fate.

Let us pause here and consider the following: Imagine two seeds that have been planted into the same soil, watered with the same water and given the same fertilizer, but one gives a shoot of wheat while the other is barley. One is sweet and the other bitter, whereas both have grown in the same soil and been subject to the same conditions. This is where 'programming' comes into the picture. One is programmed to be wheat, the other is programmed to be barley. This programming is what is commonly referred to as '*fitrah*' or one's natural disposition.

The natural disposition of an individual is basically how and why it has been created and programmed to reflect and manifest certain qualities. All seeds are fed and nourished with exactly what they need until they grow and develop to fulfill the function for which they have been created. The point at which these manifestations come to an end will mark the highest point of its evolution, at which point its sustenance will cease, and it will begin its journey back to its origin.

"Everyone acts according to his own creation program (natural disposition; *fitrah*)**."**[36]

"Indeed, We have created everything with its program (*qadar* – fate)**."**[37]

One of the other mysteries to learn at this station is about whether it is *fitrah* that determines one's fate or fate that determines one's *fitrah*. Or, in other words, is it knowledge that enables something to be known, or is it the knowing that leads to knowledge. Thus you will reflect the verse:

"You were certainly unaware of this (you were living in your cocoon)**, and We have removed from you your veil, so your sight, from this period on, is sharp."**[38]

And:

"And He is with you (the origin of your being) **wherever you are** (as your reality exists with His Names)**..."**[39]

But beware! Maintain your humility for there are innumerable Truths of which you are yet unaware; your knowledge is still inadequate. So, contemplate on this and present your impotence to your Creator.

The Rasul of Allah (saw) asked forgiveness seventy times a day for even he knew he had not comprehended the essence of the Absolute Essence, which is evidently impossible.

Thus we say:

"My Rabb, increase my knowledge."[40]

And refrain from concealed duality and wrongful assumptions. No thought, conception, idea or knowledge can ever encompass Him!

---

[36] Quran 17:84
[37] Quran 54:49
[38] Quran 50:22
[39] Quran 57:4
[40] Quran 20:114

"Vision (sense perception) **perceives Him not but He perceives** (evaluates) **all that is visible."**[41]

That is, no created entity can perceive the Creator. Is it possible for an artwork to perceive its artist?

The external is internal and the internal is external! The idea that the two are different is a misperception, an erroneous assumption due to the incapacity of the eye. We call the perceivable part of a thing 'external' and the unperceivable aspect 'internal', whereas they are in reference to the same thing! It is the eye that separates them into two different things. In reality everything is a unified whole constantly reflecting and manifesting the qualities of the One. And when all the manifestations come to an end, only Allah will remain. And even this transpires at every instance. Existence belongs to its owner. All seemingly perceivable forms are the projections of the eyes.

Whose is the sovereignty? The One who will bring all reflections to an end!

All of these are observations made as a result of the command, **"Die before you die!"**[42]

Dear reader...

If you cannot do something on your own then seek a learned one, one who has reached the essence! The fountain will not come to you if you are thirsty, you must seek it out! It will show you the way!

"Indeed, We have adorned earth's heaven (configured man's brain) **with planets** (astrological data) **and protected it** (earth's atmosphere) **from every rebellious Satan** (the purified consciousness is beyond the reach of illusory impulses)."[43]

Those who have reached the essence are like the stars; they are the stars of the heaven of contemplation! They are protected from satanic impulses, vested interests and bad thoughts, and are settled in stations that

---

[41] Quran 6:103
[42] The Bezels Of Wisdom, Ibn Arabi
[43] Quran 37:6-7

even the jinn cannot reach. They have become the protected friends of Allah.

So, correct and stabilize your path with one of them.

"And He leads to the reality by the (Names comprising the essence of the) **stars** (the people of the reality, the hadith: 'My Companions are like the stars; whoever among them you follow, you will reach the truth')...!"[44]

So, if you can't find the path then seek the stars and follow them... Let your guide be the Rasul, your master be the Quran, and your connection be to the Absolute Truth.

But remember, no mortal can be an absolute master! At most they can be the successors of the Rasul of Allah (saw), and even this is only possible for those who reflect his character.

"No more is the Rasul bound to do except provide the knowledge (of the reality and its requisites)."[45]

Ibn Arabi talks about this Truth in his *Bezels of Wisdom*. How can one dare claim to be a master when he is no more than a warner, an informer, a giver of good news and a witness?

I find it fascinating that people can make such claims when the Quran does not address them as a master (*murshid*) and even the Rasul of Allah (saw) never made such claims!

It strikes me to see people who cannot even forego their smoking habit to claim mastership and take the role of the Quran upon themselves!

Indeed, we live in a time in which blind men are describing an elephant.

But let it be known that the time has come for all paths to merge!

Soon enough those addressed by the verse **"O wrapped one"**[46] will become apparent and the claimers will become evident.

---

[44] Quran 16:16
[45] Quran 5:99
[46] Quran 74:1

Dear reader...

Seek the one who knows, one who has reached the essence, but do not become dependent on anyone! Rely only on the Rasul of Allah (saw), connect to his spirit, and take the Quran as your master and ALLAH as your friend.

The giver, whether directly or indirectly, is always Him. If the Rabb wills to give something none can prevent it. If the Rabb has not ordained something for you, then even if the entire creation comes together, they cannot give it to you.

If they can, it is only because it has been predestined for you. Every given thing is a divine reflection; you will not die until all the reflections destined for you reach you. Try and comprehend this!

Dear reader...

Words and forms are the burdens of the created.

The created give values to creation according to words and forms and appearances. But Allah is far beyond all of these. He looks not to your words and actions, but to your heart and intentions. Whether you raise your voice or secretly think of something, it is the same for Allah:

"And if you speak your thoughts (or conceal them) **know that indeed He knows the secret** (in your consciousness) **and what is even deeper** (the actual Names that compose it)."**[47]**

So, contemplate according to this... Think about creation in this light... Do not see anyone inferior to yourself, nor think you are superior to anyone...

You are a divine reflection just like everything else. He willed to manifest in a specific form in one place, and in a different form in another place. None can question Him as to why He does what He does.

"He is not questioned (called to account) **for what He does!"**[48]

---

[47] Quran 20:7
[48] Quran 21:23

Some assert there is a hadith along the lines, "Your existence is a sin that no other sin can be compared to"… The word existence in this context is in reference to the illusory identity, the ego who thinks it has a separate existence to Allah. In other words, assuming you have a separate existence, and thus causing duality, is the greatest sin.

For in Truth, your existence is a reflection of the divine. He manifests Himself every instance in yet another way. Every moment of your life is another reflection, a manifestation of the divine. So how can you, your physical biological life, be a sin?

Dear reader, know that…

Allah has created the worlds in His knowledge.

All reflections and manifestations pertain to Him. The return is to Him!

You too will return to Him when the time comes for the manifestations to end. But how?

Surely you have heard the command "Die before you die". This means, "Become aware of your essential reality before you are forced to do so."

The world is the prison for the believer! When the believer dies he is freed from this prison. So, pass through the passage of death willingly and reach eternal bliss and happiness! Eternal bliss and happiness lies beyond death. So, what are you waiting for?

If you're asking, "But how can I willingly die?" I say, by abandoning your illusory self and all your ambitions and desires! Be like a corpse who no longer has any desires. Stop wanting things and be pleased with your state. Indeed, contentment is an elevated station.

"Well-pleased is Allah with them, and well-pleased are they with Him (the reflections of divine qualities)**... This is for he who is in awe of his Rabb!"**[49]

---

[49] Quran 98:8

Neither seek the world or the hereafter. Let your only concern be to be in service to the trusts of your Rabb and to be a cause for good to reach others.

If you want to pray let your prayer be, "My Rabb, make me a vehicle for your good, make me of those you choose for yourself", so that good may occur through your hands and mouth.

When you are doing something ask yourself, "Why am I doing this?" Check to see if your answer is "For Allah" or "For myself"… The inclination of your heart will reveal your true intention. It is no use to claim your intention is one thing while your heart's desire is something else, even though you may deceive yourself into believing it…

"Actions are according to intentions" says the Rasul of Allah (saw)… And he also says, "The intention of a believer is better than his actions"… So, take this seriously until you can ask yourself, "Why am I doing this?" and your answer is "Because my Rabb wants me to "… But know, even this state will be temporary. If you are of the qualified, after some time there will be neither intention left nor any thoughts… You will go with the flow, not knowing or needing to know where you are going, only becoming aware as things transpire.

Then you will reach a state in which you will know that the doer, behind all seeming doers, is Him alone… Words will be insufficient from this point on.

Before this you were able to say, "I" or "You" or "We", but in this station such words will not hold different meanings – all of it will point to the same reality.

You will know then the ground on which you walk is not the same ground upon which you walked before…

"During that period the earth (the body) **will be replaced by another earth** (another body) **and the heavens as well** (individual consciousness will also be turned into another system of perception)!"**[50]

---

[50] Quran 14:48

Dear reader...

Junayd al-Baghdadi (s) once said, "Water takes the color of its cup"... This is when you will begin to understand what he actually meant. Water takes its shape, taste and color from the cup in which it is placed. According to the nature of the cup, the water changes in taste, shape and color.

"You were certainly unaware of this (you were living in your cocoon)**, and We have removed from you your veil, so your sight, from this period on, is sharp."**[51]

This is the station at which this verse will manifest and you will begin to observe the Truth.

Dear reader, know that...

The Truth is always the same Truth... The only thing that changes is the level of comprehension of its observers...

Water is always the same water, what changes is the tap...

Learn about water, but try also to discern its essence!

If you have been shown the ocean, do not deny that which is in the cup; if you have been shown that which is in the pot, do not deny that which is in the steam; if you have been shown the steam, do not deny the cloud... Though the names and forms may vary, their essence is the same.

Try to acquire as much knowledge from as few words as possible so that you may reach maturity quickly.

But know that nobody has ever reached the end of the road, except those who have become droplets in the ocean. Never say "I'm in the lake, I'm safe", instead attempt to reach the river and then the ocean so you may also become a droplet. For many lakes and ponds have dried up and disappeared in the past, but never has an ocean disappeared.

If you try to record what you see there, even if all the oceans and their like were to become ink, all of it will be exhausted before a single word

---

[51] Quran 50:22

is written – no hand nor mouth nor consciousness are sufficient to comprehend them.

If, after this experience of dissolution you are given a duty and must go back, everything will fall back into place, you will have to start saying 'I' and 'you' once again, but this time you will know who you are actually addressing.

Dear reader…

Never judge anyone or anything by its appearance lest you be deceived!

Satan only saw Adam's exterior and fell into the heedless mistake of judging him according to that.

He said, "He has been created from earth while I have been created from fire… Fire is superior to earth, therefore, I am superior to Adam" and refused to prostrate to Adam.

Despite all his knowledge, he failed to recognize that Allah had given a sublime Truth to Adam, of which he was devoid and unaware, and he denied his failure to recognize this.

Whereas Allah had said:

"So, when I have proportioned him (formed his brain) **and breathed into him** (manifested through him; the word 'breath' which is '*nafh*' in Arabic literally means to blow out, i.e. to project explicitly, to manifest, to materialize) **of My spirit** (My Names)…"[52]

Satan was essentially asked to surpass outward appearances and while seemingly prostrating to Adam, to actually prostrate to Allah. But he could not accept what he could not see. He confined things to only that which was visible to him and denied the possibility of things outside his perception capacity. Thus he became a disbeliever, or a coverer of the Truth.

---

[52] Quran 38:72

Only one who is unaware of the Truth or one who wants to protect the Truth from those who may abuse and exploit it will cover the Truth. While both of these cases entail an act of covering, the former is an act of disbelief and the latter stems from absolute awareness and pertains to the Nabis and the Truthful ones.

So, never deny anything that your mind can't comprehend. Only say:

"We believe, all of it is from our Rabb."[53]

And try to be of the intimates of the reality; those who have reached the essence.

Know that the one who implements his knowledge is not the one who hears, reads and learns, but the one who comprehends.

There are many people who have heard of the Truth or read the works of enlightened masters; however, being devoid of comprehension, they have failed to discern the reality, and hence sought to deny, even blame and accuse.

Do not be an imitator, but an implementer.

Do not be a narrator, but one who is narrated.

Dear reader...

It is said, **"My saints are under my dome, none knows who they are"**... Do you know who they are?

There are some servants who have abstained from the world and the hereafter; they have dived into the depths of the ocean and become droplets.

They have become "moralized with the morals of Allah" and they no longer have any concerns of wanting or not wanting.

When their Rabb asks them, "What would you like?" They answer, "Whatever you will," for they have discerned in the previous stages that even to want 'not to want' is a form of wanting! Even this, they forgo.

---

[53] Quran 3:7

Can a drop ask the ocean to take it here and there? It simply goes wherever the waves take it. If the reality is the ocean, can we say the waves are the manifestations, the reflections of the divine?

These are people who live as the reflections of divine grace for the rest of creation. Grace reaches creation through them.

"Indeed, the grace of Allah is near the doers of good (the grace of Allah reaches you by the hand that delivers it).**"**[54]

They neither harm others nor are harmed by them. They go if you ask them to go and come if you ask them to come. Even if you were to dismiss them seventy times then ask them to come, they will come without any grudge or heartache. They are the giving hands of the Rabb; they do not take. If you were to give them a gift, they would give it out to others.

They refrain from fame and status and all sorts of labels…

They ask people to follow the Rasul of Allah (saw) and take only the Quran as master.

If you ask them a question, they will answer according to the recommendation, **"Address people according to their level of intellect."**[55]

They are like a mirror – whoever looks at them sees themselves. The faults and mistakes they see on them will be their own faults and mistakes.

If you are like all the other people of your time, you will see them, the saints, no different to yourself. If you are of the people seeking the hereafter, who fear punishment and desire pleasure, again, you will see them in the same way. And if you are neither of these, but one who has gone beyond both, again you will find them at your station of arrival… This is one of the divine veils preventing them from being recognized. The other is their physical form and appearance.

Because the majority of people cannot transgress a set level of comprehension, they are unable to think about the innumerable forms of creation outside their perception range, they judge according to what they see. Thus, with such judgments, they deceive themselves. But this

---

[54] Quran 7:56
[55] Sahih Muslim, Abu Dawood

actually serves them. Their dress code, lifestyle, environment and the way they appear does not in any way give the impression that they are saints. They do not need to show and reveal themselves.

Most of them have attained insight into the mystery of fate. Hence, they do not busy themselves with others. Even the Nabi are informed of the mystery of fate after some time into their *Nubuwwah*, in order that they may be able to fully fulfill their duty.

If you are thirsty for the Truth, seek them and, despite all impediments, try to get to know them… Become like them so that the way to becoming 'moralized with the morals of Allah' opens to you.

They are the people of '*Fardiyyah*'! They only follow the Rasul and their Rabb. None can interfere. They know and recognize each other and oftentimes meet. But they are aware that they are all manifestations of the same reality.

They are those to whom Rasulullah (saw) refers with his words, "The *mufarrid* (the people of *Fardiyyah*) have surpassed you" when talking with his disciples.

They neither follow a particular path or a school of thought.

Like Ghazali (salam upon him) who placed the Quran on his chest before passing away and said, "This is my school", they also live by this Truth.

They have come into form and they have 'died' of their illusory identities, and thus they no longer think or fret about death… For they will not taste death again…

"They will not taste death therein except the first death (they are immortal)**! And He will have protected them from the suffering of burning."**[56]

They have long tasted death and have moved on to the realms of bliss, paradise. They are busy with the observation of their Rabb… At every instance they are in contact with their Rabb… Thus are the saints, the truthful, the *mufarridoon*, hidden beneath the veil of the Rabb.

---

[56] Quran 44:56

Dear reader...

The Rasul of Allah (saw) was asked, "Who are the *mufarridoon*?" He answered, "Those who remember Allah frequently!"

Know that there is not a single creation that does not exalt (*tasbih*) Allah:

"There is nothing that does not exalt (*tasbih*) **Him with** *hamd* (evaluation of the corporeal worlds created with His Names, as He wills)! **But you do not perceive their functions! Indeed, He is the Halim, the Ghafur."**[57]

The entire creation is constantly glorifying and exalting Him. Some knowingly, some unknowingly... Humans, animals, stones, the mountains, plants, the air... everything! But those to whom divine knowledge has not been bestowed will not be aware of this.

The exaltation (*tasbih*) of every manifestation of a Name, every divine reflection is its materialization and the purpose behind its creation. If you are of the qualified you will try to discern this. The Rabb is the Creator of the reflections that He wills to reflect.

It's important to note that in the attempt to describe the *mufarridoon* it is not said they engage in exaltation (*tasbih*) or that they are patient or that they engage in *hamd*, but rather that "they remember (*dhikr*) Allah frequently."

"Remember Allah while standing, sitting, or (lying) **on your sides** (i.e. experience Him in your being at all times)..."[58]

The exaltation of creation in general is different to that of man. This one is in reference to man as evident in the following verse:

"Indeed, we offered the Trust (living consciously of the Names) **to the heavens** (consciousness of the self, ego) **and the earth** (the body) **and the mountains** (the organs), **and they declined to bear it** (their Name compositions did not have the capacity to manifest it) **and feared**

---

[57] Quran 17:44
[58] Quran 4:103

it; but Man (the consciousness to manifest the Names that compose vicegerency) **undertook to bear it...**"[59]

The effect of *dhikr* changes according to the state and elevation of the people. In the beginning it is done as mere vocal repetitions, but after some time it becomes the practice of the heart, rather than the tongue. In other words 'contemplative *dhikr*' is the first step of real *dhikr*, the stages prior to this serve as steps leading here.

Here are some hadith relevant to this topic:

"An hour of contemplation is better than a year of worship."

"An hour of contemplation is better than seventy years of worship."

"An hour of contemplation is better than a thousand years of worship."[60]

When a person begins to contemplate he leaves this world... After this, his *dhikr* derives from the unknown (observing the Names in terms of their essence)... He no longer has any ties to the afterlife.

After this stage, 'hidden' (*hafi*) *dhikr* begins! Here, contemplation is even isolated from the meanings of the Names. This is the station of Absolute Oneness, Absolute Inseparableness that is contemplated and observed.

The station after this is that of the even more hidden (*ahfa*) *dhikr*. Neither words nor the pen has the power to say anything about this station. The Rabb knows it. It is with the Rabb, from the Rabb. It is the Rabb!

When a person begins to engage in the remembrance with the spiritual state of this mystery, it means he becomes wrapped with the veil of the Rabb. This is the kind of contemplation that the Rasul (saw) claims is better than a thousand years of worship. The other hadith are in relevance to the stages before this. As Bayazid al-Bastami said: "When I was at the beginning of the journey they called me 'devout'; when I neared the end they called me 'an atheist'!"

---

[59] Quran 33:72
[60] Quran 97:3; Sirr al-Asrar wa Mazhar al-Anwar , Abdul-Qadir Gilani

Be aware that it is crucially important not to abandon the physical-external aspect of the commands, for the Rasul of Allah (saw) never did! There is important scientific truth in the recommended practices of worship, which I have covered in *The Mystery of Man*.

Those who call Bayazid an atheist are like people who have a Geiger counter, a handheld device that measures radioactivity, trying to measure the radioactivity of a massive field, but the counter shows only a bunch of zeroes. Hence they deduce, 'There is no radioactive material here". But one among them who knows better says, "Perhaps there is radiation here, but at a level a lot higher than we assume. We may need a stronger device." So they update their device and measure again only to discover the radioactivity level is significantly higher than their assumption.

Thus, those who are deprived of this knowledge always criticize or deny ideas and people fall outside the range of their own capacity. This is the primary reason of critical approach and denial. Man denies what he cannot comprehend. And to those who say, "If this is so how do we take others as examples?" we say:

Take only our Rasul (saw) as an example, and take only the Quran as a master. The Quran binds you only to follow the Rasul (saw).

Criticizing or denying people who you are unable to understand only reveals your lack of discretion and comprehension. In any case, they are free from your judgments...

So obey the verse:

"Remember (*dhikr*) Him to the degree of your realization of your essential reality"[61]

Turn to the Truth and try to attain discernment. Surely you can only do this according to your capacity, so why deny those who have a greater capacity than yours? Everyone's responsibility is in accordance to their capacity:

"Allah will never hold anyone responsible for that which they have no capacity."[62]

---

[61] Quran 2:198
[62] Quran 2:286

Dear reader…

Those who inquired about the spirit were told:

"…Say 'The spirit is from the command of my Rabb (*amr*; the manifestation of the Names). **And you have been given little of this knowledge** (this answer is for the Jews who asked this question)'…"[63]

And:

"So when I have proportioned him (formed his brain) **and breathed into him** (manifested through him; the word 'breath' which is '*nafh*' in Arabic literally means to blow out, i.e. to project explicitly, to manifest, to materialize) **of My spirit** (My Names)…"[64]

In one of the hadith, the Rasul of Allah uses the word 'Ruhullah' (the Spirit of Allah).

As can be seen the verse above begins with the command 'Say', addressing the Rasul of Allah (saw), to mean "Narrate what I'm about to tell you to the Jews who are making this inquiry"… Surely, the Rasul of Allah (saw) knew what the spirit was, but those who made the inquiry were unaware of its Truth. Moreover, they were with the impression that the Truth of the spirit can never be known!

Due to this the Rasul (saw) refrained from answering their question and sought the knowledge of His Rabb instead… Which was evidently the most appropriate action to take.

If he had given the impression that he didn't know, they would have mocked and ridiculed him. If he had explained its Truth to them, they would not have been able to understand it and denied this knowledge, which had not been previously given to them.

So the Rabb reflected according to their assumption and gave a short concise answer, "The spirit is from the command of my Rabb" and added, "You have been given little of this knowledge."

---

[63] Quran 17:85
[64] Quran 38:72

In other words, due to your incapacity to comprehend the Truth regarding the spirit you have been given little knowledge of it, lest you seek denial.

Having said this, the spirit is the manifestation of your Rabb's command. This being the case, sickness, defect, corruption, etc., are rendered invalid. The spirit cannot be in pain or pleasure! All of these emanate from the brain.

"The spirit is the command of Allah" just like Gabriel; a form of consciousness from the realm of divine command (*amr*). We all know that the angels neither eat nor drink, or feel tired, sleep, nor can they be labeled as good or bad, sick or healthy! Even the concept of gender is invalid in this realm. So, how can anyone say such things about the spirit, which is also from the command of the Rabb?

The Spirit is One, it is the source of life. It is the essential element comprising our being; the Grand Spirit! There is also the personal spirit, which is formed by the brain. Detailed information on the Grand Spirit and the personal spirit has been covered in *Spirit Man Jinn* and *The Human Enigma*.

All allegations made in regards to this topic stem from the brain. The command of the Rabb is beyond all of this. Thus a spirit cannot be called or evoked. Only the Rabb can call a spirit, at which point the spirit will leave its body and return to its origin.

All claims made about the spirit are reflections of the natural disposition, which on the physical level, project from the brain.

Neither the Rasul (saw) nor the saints and scholars that came after him have ever made such allegations. A few who were made to say something about this topic in later generations narrated their own experiences, which has reached our times.

Our duty is to explain the truth with the permission of the Rabb. Doubtlessly, everyone can only talk according to their level of knowledge.

It is evident that beyond a learned one is one who is more learned.

So, dear reader...

I have tried to share some knowledge with you in this short book. Like I said in the beginning, each person will benefit according to his or her creational program, capacity and level of comprehension. Each person will benefit according to the guidance given by his or her Rabb.

It was willed, so it was written!

The Rabb is He who will preserve it and allow it to be understood.

I seek refuge in Allah from all my mistaken assumptions and admit my impotence to duly gratify Him.

Hamd belongs to Allah, the Rabb of the worlds!

Allah is great!

AHMED HULUSI

21.1.1967
Cerrahpasha - Istanbul

ABOUT THE AUTHOR

Ahmed Hulusi (Born January 21, 1945, Istanbul, Turkey) contemporary Islamic philosopher. From 1965 to this day he has written close to 30 books. His books are written based on Sufi wisdom and explain Islam through scientific principles. His established belief that the knowledge of Allah can only be properly shared without any expectation of return has led him to offer all of his works which include books, articles, and videos free of charge via his web-site. In 1970 he started examining the art of spirit evocation and linked these subjects parallel references in the Quran (smokeless flames and flames instilling pores). He found that these references were in fact pointing to luminous energy which led him to write *Spirit, Man, Jinn* while working as a journalist for the Aksam newspaper in Turkey. Published in 1985, his work called *The Human Enigma (Insan ve Sirlari)* was Hulusi's first foray into decoding the messages of the Quran filled with metaphors and examples through a scientific backdrop. In 1991 he published *The Power of Prayer (Dua and Zikir)* where he explains how the repetition of certain prayers and words can lead to the realization of the divine attributes inherent within our essence through increased brain capacity. In 2009 he completed his final work, '*Decoding the Quran, A Unique Sufi Interpretation*' which encompasses the understanding of leading Sufi scholars such as Abdulkarim al Jili, Abdul-Qadir Jilani, Muhyiddin Ibn al-Arabi, Imam Rabbani, Ahmed ar-Rifai, Imam Ghazali, and Razi, and which approached the messages of the Quran through the secret Key of the letter 'B'.

GLOSSARY OF SUFI TERMS

Al-Adl: The One who provides each of His manifestations their due right in consonance with their creation program. The One who is absolutely free from unjustness or tyranny.

Al-Afuw: The One who forgives all offences except for 'duality' (*shirq*); the failure to recognize the reality of non-duality prevents the activation of the name *al-Afuw*.

Ahadiyyah: The absolute oneness of existence.

Ahlul Haqiqah: The intimates of the reality.

Ahlul Tahqiq: The people of authenticity.

Al-Akhir: The infinitely subsequent One, to all creation.

Al-Aleem: The One who, with the quality of His knowledge, infinitely knows everything in every dimension with all its facets.

Al-Aliy: The Highest (or the Sublime). The sublime One who observes existence from the point of reality (essence).

Allah: ALLAH... Such a name... It points to *Uluhiyyah*!

Uluhiyyah encompasses two realities. HU which denotes Absolute Essence (*dhat*) and the realm of infinite points in which every single point is formed by the act of observing knowledge through knowledge. This act of observing is such that each point signifies an individual composition of Names.

Aql al-Awwal: The First Intellect; the first disclosure of universal consciousness.

Aql al-Qull: The Universal Intellect; universal consciousness.

Arsh: Throne. Denotes universal prolificacy, though not in terms of the perceived material world.

Ashraf al-Mahluq: The most honored of all creation.

Al-Awwal: The first and initial state of existence, the essential Name.

Al-Aziz: The One who, with His unchallengeable might, disposes as He wishes. The One whose will to do as He likes, nothing can oppose. This name works in parallel with the name *Rabb*. The *Rabb* attribute carries out the demands of the Aziz attribute!

Al-Azim: The magnificent glory beyond any manifestation's capacity of comprehension.

41

Al-Badee:	The incomparable beauty and the originator of beautiful manifestation! The One who originates innumerable manifestations, all with unique and exclusive qualities, and without any example, pattern, specimen etc.
Al-Baith:	The One who constantly transforms new dimensions of existence.
Al-Basit:	The One who opens and expands; the One who enables dimensional and in-depth sight.
Al-Basir:	The One who is constantly observing His manifestations and evaluating their outputs.
Al-Bari:	The One who fashions all of creation (from micro to macro) with unique functions and designs yet all in conformity with the whole, like the harmonious functioning of all the different organs in the body!
Al-Barr:	The One who eases the actualization of individual temperaments and natural dispositions.
Al-Batin:	The unperceivable reality within the perceivable manifestation! The source of the unknown (*Awwal, Akhir, Zahir, Batin, HU!*)
Al-Baqi:	The Everlasting. The One who exists beyond the concept of time.
Barzakh:	The intermediary dimension.
B-izni-hi (by permission of Allah):	The suitability of the Name composition comprising his essence.
Ad-Darr:	The One who afflicts individuals with various distressing situations (sickness, suffering, trouble) in order to make them turn to Himself!
D'hul Fadhlul Azim:	Possessor of great bounty.
D'hul-Jalali Wal-ikram:	The One who makes individuals experience their 'nothingness' by enabling them to comprehend the reality that they were created from 'naught' and then bestowing them 'Eternity' by allowing them to observe the manifestations of the Names comprising their essence.
Dhu'l Quwwati'l Matin:	Possessor of enduring strength.
Arham-ar-rahimeen:	The One who manifests the infinite qualities of His Names with His grace.
Fath:	Self-conquest.
Al-Fattah:	The One who generates expansion within individuals. The One who enables the recognition and observation of Reality, and hence, that there is no inadequacy, impairment, or mistake in the engendered existence. The

42

	One who expands one's vision and activity, and enables their proper usage. The One who enables the recognition and use of the unrecognized (overseen).
Fuad:	Heart - heart neurons. The reflectors of the Names to the brain.
Furqan:	The ability and knowledge to differentiate the right from the wrong or the criterion by which the reality may be differentiated from falsity.
Gabriel:	The disclosure of the knowledge of Allah.
Al-Gaffar:	The One who, as requisites of divine power or wisdom, 'conceals' the inadequacies of those who recognize their shortcomings and wish to be freed from their consequences. The One who forgives.
Al-Ghafur:	The One who's Mercy should never be doubted or given up on. The One who enables necessary cleansing and triggers the name *Rahim* to bestow blessings.
Al-Ghani:	The One who is beyond being labeled and limited by the manifestations of His Names, as He is Great (Akbar) and beyond all concepts. The One who is infinitely abundant with His Names.
Al-Habir:	The One who is aware of the manifestations of His Names at all times. The One who allows his manifestations to discern the level of their comprehension via their outputs.
Al-Hadi:	The guide to the truth. The One who allows individuals to live according to their reality. The articulator of the truth. The guide to reality.
Al-Hafiz:	The One who provides all requirements to preserve and maintain existence.
Al-Hakam:	The Absolute Judge whose judgment (verdict) is irresistibly applied.
Al-Hakim:	The One whose power of knowledge appears under the guise of 'causes', hence creating causality and leading to the perception of multiplicity.
Al-Halim:	The One who refrains from giving sudden (impulsive) reactions to events, but rather evaluates all situations in respect of their purpose of manifestation.
Hamd:	The evaluation of the corporeal worlds created with His Names, as He wills.

Al-Hamid:	The One who observes and evaluates His universal perfection on worldly forms manifested by His Name *al-Waliyy*.
Al-Haqq:	The absolute and unequivocal reality! The source and essence of every function in manifestation!
Al-Hasib:	The One who maintains individuality by holding them to account of their behavioral output through the mechanics of 'consequence'.
Al-Hayy:	The source of names! The One who gives life to the Names and manifests them. The source of universal energy, the essence of energy!
Hu:	Whether via revelation or through consciousness, HU is the inner essence of the reality of everything that is perceived... To such extent that, as the reflection of *Akbariyyah*, first awe then nothingness is experienced and, as such, the Reality of Hu can never be attained! Sight cannot reach HU! HU denotes absolute obscurity and incomprehension! As a matter of fact, all names, including Allah are mentioned in connection with HU in the Quran!
Huda:	Guidance; enabling the comprehension of one's essential reality.
Ind'Allah:	From Allah; the forces that are revealed through dimensional emergence to consciousness from the Names of Allah that comprise one's essence.
Insan al-Kamil:	The Perfect Man.
Isra:	The supersensible and dimensional travel by night.
Al-Jabbar:	The One whose will is compelling. The corporeal worlds (engendered existence) are compelled to comply with His demands! There is no room for refusal. This *'jabr'* (compelling) quality will inevitably express itself and apply its laws through the essence of beings.
Al-Jalil:	The One who, with His magnificent comprehensiveness and perfection, is the sultan of the world of acts.
Al-Jami:	The One who observes the whole of existence as a multi-dimensional single frame in His Knowledge. The One who gathers creation according to the purpose and function of their creation.
Al-Kabir:	The magnitude of the worlds He created with His Names are incomprehensible.
Kashf al-Nurani:	Enlightened discovery.
Kashf al-Dhulmani:	Purification through suffering.

44

Al-Karim:	The exceedingly generous and bountiful One who bestows His bounties even upon those who deny His existence. The ability to READ (*iqra*) is only possible through the activation of this Name, which lies dormant within the essence of every individual.
Al-Khafid:	The One who abases. The One who capacitates a state of existence which is far from reality. The creator of the '*asfali safileen*' (the lower state of existence). The former of the vision of **'multiplicity'** to conceal the reality.
Al-Khaliq:	The ONE Absolute Creator! The One who brings individuals into the existence from nothingness, with His Names! Everything *al-Khaliq* creates has a purpose to fulfill, and according to this unique purpose, possesses a natural predisposition and character. Hence it has been said: "characterize yourselves with the character of Allah" (Tahallaku biakhlakillah) to mean: Live in accordance with the awareness that you are comprised of the structural qualities of the Names of Allah!
Kitab al-Mubin:	The Clear Book.
Kursi:	Footstool – the actualization and dominance of the reality of the Names.
Ladun:	The potential of the Names comprising one's essence.
Al-Latif:	The One who is subtly present in the depths of every manifestation. The One whose favors are plentiful.
Al-Maalik'ul-Mulk:	The One who governs His Sovereignty as He wishes without having to give account to any individual.
Mahshar:	The place of gathering.
Maiyyah:	Unity of existence.
Al-Majeed:	The One whose majestic glory is evident through His magnificent manifestations!
Al-Majid:	The magnificent and glorious One with unrestricted, infinite generosity and endowment (benevolence).
Mala-i A'la:	The Exalted Assembly.
Al-Maleek:	The Sovereign One, who manifests His Names as he wishes and governs them in the world of acts as He pleases. The one who has providence over all things.
Al-Mani:	The One who prevents those from attaining things they do not deserve!
Manna:	The force of power in the names of Allah comprising your essence.
Marifah:	Gnosis.

Al-Matin:	The One who sustains the world of acts, the steadfast, the creator of robustness and stability, the provider of strength and resistance!
Mawla:	Protector.
Michael:	The force that guides to and enables the attainment of both physical and spiritual sustenance.
Al-Mu'akhkhir:	The One who delays manifestation in consonance with His name *al-Hakim*.
Al-Mubdi:	The One who originates the whole of creation in the corporeal worlds, all with exclusive and unique qualities.
Al-Mudhill:	The One who exposes dishonor in some and degrades below others. The One who deprives from honorable qualities and compels to humiliation with the veil of 'I'ness (ego).
Al-Mughni:	The One who enriches individuals and raises them above others in wealth and emancipates them. The One who enriches with His own riches. The One who grants the beauty of infinity (*baqa*) which results from '*fakr*' (nothingness).
Al-Muhaymin	The One who maintains and protects the manifestations of His Names with His own system. *Al-Muhaymin* also designates the One who safeguards and protects (the trust).
Al-Muhsi:	The creator of the 'forms' (micro to macro) comprising the seeming multiplicities, each equipped with unique qualities and attributes, within UNITY.
Al-Muhyi:	The One who enlivens and enlightens! The One who enables the continuation of the individual's life through the application of knowledge and the observation of one's essential reality.
Al-Mu'id:	The One who restores life to those who turn back to their essence.
Al-Mu'izz:	The Giver of Honor. The One who bestows honor to whom he wishes and holds them in esteem over others.
Al-Mujib:	The One who unequivocally responds to all who turn towards Him (in prayer and invocation) and provides their needs.
Al-Mu'min:	The One who enables the awareness that He, by respect of His Names, is beyond what is perceived. This awareness reflects upon us as **'faith'** (*iman*). All believers, including Rasuls and angels, have their faith rested upon this awareness, which frees the mind from the

enslavement of illusion. While illusion can deter the mind, which uses comparison to operate, it becomes powerless and ineffective in the sight of faith.

Muqarraboon:	Those who have attained the state of divine closeness.
Al-Muntaqim:	The One who makes individuals live the consequences of their actions that impede in the realization of their essence.
Al-Mumit:	The One who enables a 'taste' (experience)
Al-Mutakabbir:	The One to whom the word 'I' exclusively belongs. Absolute 'I'ness belongs only to Him. Whoever, with the word 'I', accredits a portion of this Absolute 'I'ness to himself, thereby concealing the 'I'ness comprising his essence and fortifying his own relative 'I'ness, will pay its consequence with 'burning' (suffering). Majesty (Absolute 'I'ness) is His attribute alone.
Al-Musawwir:	The fashioner of forms. The One who exhibits 'meanings' as 'forms' and devises the mechanism in the perceiver to perceive them.
Al-Muqeet:	The One who facilitates the expression of the Name *al-Hafiz* by providing the necessary material and spiritual platform for it.
Al-Muqaddim:	The One who expedites (or prioritizes) the manifestation of Names according to their purpose of creation.
Al-Muqsit:	The One who applies justice, as the requirement of His *Uluhiyya*, by endowing every individual their due, based on their unique creation purpose.
Al-Muqtadir:	The Determiner. The absolute possessor of all power pertaining to creation, governance, and disposition.
Al-Muta'ali:	The limitless, boundless Supreme One, whose supremacy encompasses everything! The One whose reality can never be duly reflected by any engendered, conceptualized existence. The One who is beyond being limited by any mind or intellect.
Muttaqeen:	Those who live in line with their essential reality.
An-Nafi:	The One who prompts individuals to engage in good thoughts and actions to aid them towards beneficent and auspicious outcomes.
Nafs:	Self, individual consciousness.
	Nafs-i Ammarah: The Inciting Self.
	Nafs-i Lawwama: The Self-Accusing Self.

	Nafs-i Mulhima: The Inspired Self.
	Nafs-i Mutmainna: The Peaceful Self.
	Nafs-i Radhiya: The Pleased Self.
	Nafs-i Mardhiya: The Pleasing Self.
	Nafs-i Safiya: The Pure Self.
Names:	Divine Names – structural and compositional qualities comprising existence.
Nubuwwah:	The function of enabling people to read and apply the necessary practices of the system of Allah.
An-Nur:	The Knowledge that is the source and essence of everything! The essence of everything is *Nur*; everything is comprised of knowledge. Life subsists with knowledge. Those with knowledge are the ever-living ones (*Hayy*), while those who lack knowledge are like living dead.
Al-Qabid:	The One who exercises His verdict by retaining the essence of an individual's Name reality. The One who restrains and enforces withdrawnness.
Al-Qadir:	The One who creates (discloses, manifests) and observes His knowledge with His power without depending on causality. The One who is absolutely boundless!
Al-Qahhar:	The One who executes the effects of His Name '*Wahid*' and renders invalid the seeming existence of the relative 'I'ness.
Al-Qayyum:	The One who renders Himself existent with His own attributes, without the need of anything. Everything in existence subsists with *al-Qayyum*.
Al-Qawwi:	The One who transforms His power into the enabling potential for the manifestation of existence (hence comprising the force of the whole of existence).
Al-Quddus:	The One who is free and beyond being defined, conditioned and limited by His manifest qualities and concepts! Albeit the engendered existence is the disclosure of His Names, He is pure and beyond from becoming defined and limited by them!
Qurbiyyah:	The state of divine closeness.
Rabb:	The Name composition/divine qualities comprising one's essence.
Ar-Rafi:	The One who exalts. The one who elevates conscious beings to higher states of existence; to enable the realization and observation of their essential reality.

Ar-Rahman:	*Ar-Rahman* signifies the materialization of the essence of every iota with Allah's Names in His knowledge. In modern terms, it designates the quantum potential. It is the potential of the source of the entire creation. It is the name of the Dimension of Names! All things obtain their existence at the level of knowledge and will with the attributes denoted by this name.
Rahmaniyyah:	The quantum potential.
Rahmah:	Grace.
Ar-Rahim:	*Ar-Rahim* is the Name that brings the infinite qualities of *ar-Rahman* into engendered existence. In this sense, it is the 'observation' of the potential. *Ar-Rahim* observes itself through the forms of existence, by guiding the conscious beings to the awareness that their lives and their essential reality are comprised of and governed by the Names.
Ar-Raqib:	The One who watches over and keeps under control the manifestations of His Names, with His names, at all times.
Ar-Rashid:	The guider to the right path. The One who allows individuals, who recognize their essential reality, to experience the maturity of this recognition!
Rasul:	One through whom the reality is disclosed - the articulation of Allah's knowledge.
Al-Ra'uf:	The compassionate and pitying One who protects individuals who turn to Him from all kinds of behavior which may cause harm or trouble to them.
Al-Razzaq:	The One who provides all necessary nutrition for the survival of any unit of manifestation regardless of its plane of existence.
Rububiyyah:	Compositional qualities denoted by the Names comprising existence.
Ruhu'l Azam:	The Grand Spirit; the observing One.
As-Salam:	A state of emancipation from the conditions
As-Sabur:	The One who waits for each individual to execute his creation program before rendering effective the consequences of their actions. Allowing the tyranny of the tyrant to take place, i.e. activating the Name *as-Sabur*, is so that both the oppressor and the oppressed can duly carry out their functions before facing the consequences in full effect. Greater calamity forces the creation of increased cruelty.

Samad/Samadiyyah:	The Absolutely Self-Sufficient and Whole One.
As-Sami:	The One who perceives His manifestations at every instance. The One who enables awareness and comprehension.
Sayr al-Afaqi:	The recognition of the universal realities.
Sayr al-Anfusi:	The recognition of the individual realities or the path of the inward journey.
Shadid al-Iqab:	Severe in enforcing the due consequence of an offence.
Ash-Shahid:	The One who witnesses His existence through His own existence. The One who observes the disclosure of His Names and witnesses His manifestations!
Ash-Shakur:	The One who allows the proper use of His bestowals in order that He may increase them. The One who enables the due evaluation of resources such that more can be attained. This name triggers the name *al-Karim*.
Shirq:	Duality – the state of assuming the separate existence of an 'other' besides Allah.
Subhan:	One who is beyond being limited or conditioned by any of His manifestations.
Sunnatullah:	The mechanics of the system of Allah.
Tanzih:	The incomparability of the divine.
Taqwa:	Protecting yourself in the way of Allah from the inadequacies of your identity.
Tasbih:	Glorify, exalt – to continue one's existence through Him.
Tashbih:	The similarity/comparability of the divine.
At-Tawwab:	The One who guides individuals to their essence by enabling them to perceive and comprehend the reality. The One who allows individuals to repent, that is, to abandon their misdoings and to compensate for any harm that may have been caused. The activation of this Name triggers the name *Rahim*, and thus benevolence and beauty is experienced.
The Divine Reflections:	
	The Hidden – Reflection of attributes.
	The Secret – Reflection of the Names.
	The Spirit – Fuad: Reflectors of the Names.
	The Heart – Consciousness.

	The Self – Identity – Individual consciousness.
Ubudiyyah:	Servitude of the 'self' or individual consciousness by means of fulfilling its specific function and purpose of creation.
Ulul Albab:	The intimates of the reality through whom Allah hears, sees and speaks.
Al-Wahhab:	The One who bestows and gives unrequitedly to those He wishes, oblivious of deservedness.
Al-Wahid:	The One and only! 'ONE'ness far beyond any concept of multiplicity. The ONE, that isn't composed of (or can be broken into) parts (as in pantheism). The 'ONE'ness that renders duality obsolete! The 'ONE'ness that no mind or intellect can fully comprehend!
Al-Wakil:	The One who provides the means for self-actualization. The One who advocates and protects those who place their trust in Him, providing them with the most auspicious outcomes.
Al-Wali:	The One who governs according to His own verdict.
Wajh:	Divine countenance.
Al-Wasi:	The All-embracing. The One who embraces the whole of existence with the expressions of His Names.
Vicegerent:	Conscious beings who will live with the awareness of the Names.
Al-Wadud:	The creator of attraction. The creator of unconditional and unrequited love. The essence within every beloved!
Al-Wajid:	The One whose qualities and attributes are unfailingly abundant. The manifest One. The One, from which nothing lessens, despite the abundance of His manifestations.
Al-Waliyy:	The One who guides and enables an individual to discover their reality and to live their life in accordance to their essence. It is the source of *risalah* (personification of Allah's knowledge) and *nubuwwah* (prophethood), which comprise the pinnacle states of sainthood (*wilayah*). It is the dispatcher of the perfected qualities comprising the highest point of sainthood, *risalah*, and the state one beneath that, *nubuwwah*.
Waliyy:	Friend, guardian/protector.
Al-Warith:	The One who manifests under various names and forms in order to inherit and protect the possessions of those

who abandon all their belongings to undergo true transformation. When one form is exhausted, He continues His existence with another form.

Yakeen:
The state of certainty; to be in complete submission as a result of an absolute comprehension.

a. The knowledge of certainty (ilm al-yakeen)

b. The eye of certainty (ayn al-yakeen)

c. The reality of certainty (haqq al-yakeen)

Az-Zahir:
The self-evident One, the explicit, unequivocal and perceivable manifestation.

Zawj:
While its most common usage is to mean 'partner in marriage' it has also been used in the context of consciousness, implying the partner or equivalent of consciousness.

www.ingramcontent.com/pod-product-compliance
Lightning Source LLC
Chambersburg PA
CBHW021918040426
42448CB00007B/806